# POLAR BEAR

# POLAR BEAR

## Kay McDearmon

*Illustrated with photographs*

DODD, MEAD & COMPANY

NEW YORK

## ACKNOWLEDGMENTS

For current material and information I am particularly grateful to Jack W. Lentfer, U.S. Fish and Wildlife Service, Anchorage, Alaska; C. R. Harington, National Museum, Ottawa, Canada; and Ian Stirling, Canadian Wildlife Service, Edmonton, Canada.

Photographs courtesy of:

Chicago Zoological Society, 30; Bob Crawford, 1; C. R. Harington, 15; Information Canada Photothèque, 34, 38; San Diego Zoo Photo, 13, 16, 21, 22, 24, 25, 26, 28, 35; U.S. Coast Guard Official Photo, 17, 45; U.S. Fish and Wildlife Service Photograph, 36; U.S. Fish and Wildlife Service Photograph by Jim Brooks, 41; U.S. Fish and Wildlife Service Photographs by Jack W. Lentfer, 2, 10, 19, 32, 43; University of Alaska Archives, Barrett Willoughby Collection, 33.

30027000023504

Library of Congress Cataloging in Publication Data

McDearmon, Kay.
    Polar bear.

    SUMMARY: Details the life cycle of the polar bear, "undisputed animal ruler of the arctic ice."
    1. Polar bear—Juvenile literature. [1. Polar bear] I. Title.
QL737.C27M27        599'.74446        76-8920
ISBN 0-396-07331-X

*To my nieces and nephews*

# INTRODUCTORY NOTE

Polar bears have been seen almost everywhere in the Arctic, even near the North Pole. However, most live at the southern edge of the sea ice where seals are more numerous. In some areas of their range the great white bears are abundant; in others, almost extinct.

Until recently it was believed that polar bears (*Ursus maritimus*) drifted clockwise all around the pole on ice floes. Now that scientists have begun to tag the bears, the sites of recapture suggest that some bears may limit their traveling to a particular region. Nevertheless, since food is often hard to find, the polar bear is constantly on the move.

For three hundred years the greatest threat to the bears has come from man. Explorers, whalers, fur traders,

7

sportsmen, and natives have hunted them. For Eskimos killing a polar bear was once a test of manhood. Altogether, estimates indicate that men have killed 150,000.

The International Union for the Conservation of Nature has labeled the polar bear "vulnerable." Fortunately, recent national laws have restricted hunting of the 12,000 that may remain. And in 1973 a treaty between the five polar bear nations—United States, Canada, Denmark, Norway, and Russia—banned polar bear hunting by airplanes or large motorized vehicles.

The environment poses still other hazards. Poisonous insecticides have been found in the tissues of polar bears captured even in remote areas. Gas and oil exploration in the Arctic is likely to force the bears to den in less desirable areas. It is feared that oil spills will harm the fish that seals eat. With fewer seals to eat, some bears will surely starve.

Scientists from the polar bear countries are now cooperating in studies they hope will help to insure the survival of this magnificent wanderer of the arctic seas.

8

# POLAR BEAR

THE March sun hung low in the sky as the big white bear poked her massive head out of her snow den. Turning back, she reached down to help her two cubs exit from their winter hideaway to face the white polar world for the first time. As the baby bears wobbled after their mother, they tried not to fall into her immense footprints in the snow.

Last October, when she was expecting the cubs, she had left the southern edge of the arctic sea ice and headed for land. Once ashore, she searched for a snowbank on the slope of a hill.

There she scooped out a den and enlarged it until it was about seven feet long, five feet wide, and four feet high. Finally, blizzards sealed the opening. The air the bear needed, and a tiny amount of light, came through a small hole she punched in the snow roof.

While she slept, snug in her dark den, her temperature dropped only a few degrees, her heart kept pumping in almost normal fashion, and she awakened easily.

In the coldest part of the long arctic winter she awakened to give birth to the cubs. They were born blind, deaf, and almost without fur. At birth they were only ten inches long, and weighed less than two pounds. They were so tiny and so helpless that their 500-pound mother had to be careful not to crush them.

Like their full-grown mother, they slept most of the time, awakening only to suckle her warm, rich milk. Then they snuggled back into her soft, dense fur. For six weeks they couldn't see their mother. Soon after they began crawling around; a month or so later they were climbing—still safely inside the den.

Now in late March as they scrambled outside the den for the first time after their mother, the cubs weighed

nearly twenty pounds and looked like small, woolly white dogs. As the cubs glanced around, the glare from the ice and snow didn't bother them at all. An extra membrane that acted like sunglasses protected their small, black eyes.

The bears wandered a short distance, then they stopped and played together on the snowy slope. The cubs slid down on their rumps, sometimes going so fast that they flipped over. When they reached the bottom, their mother caught them. Over and over they climbed up the hill and slid down again.

After the cubs wrestled for awhile, the bear family began meandering again. Along the way the mother searched for food. For five months she had fasted in her den, living off her reserves of fat, and now she was lean and hungry. With her sharp claws she dug up frozen grasses and berries and nibbled on them.

The bears didn't travel far from their den that day or for several days. Still, sometimes the baby bears became tired. Then their mother let them ride on her back. Or she dug a pit in the snow, sheltered from the wind, and they all slept there for hours. Each night they returned to the den.

Outside it was freezing, but the piled-up snow and the mother's body heat kept their igloo-like cave about forty degrees warmer inside.

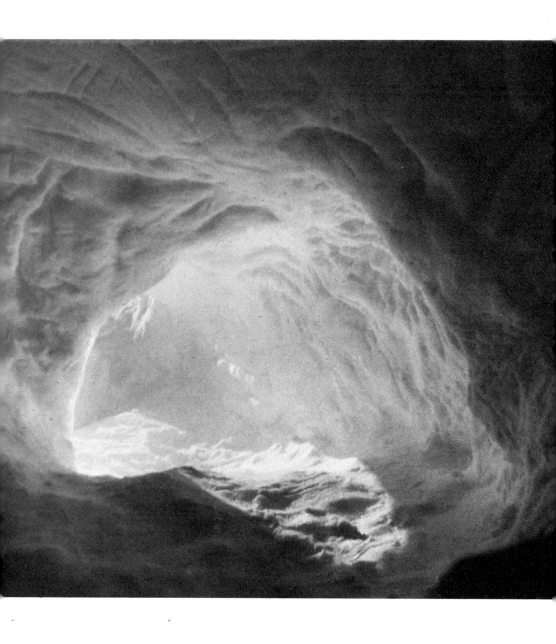

One day in early April the polar bears left their snow den for the season and shuffled off toward the drifting sea ice to hunt seals, their favorite food.

They had not gone far when they saw a giant polar bear coming toward them. He was at least four hundred pounds heavier than the mother bear, and standing on his hind legs he would tower ten feet high.

He could be the cubs' father. They wouldn't know, for they had never seen him. Last spring their father had followed their mother's tracks on the sea ice. A few days after they had met and mated, he deserted her to search for another female.

Right now the cubs' mother wasn't at all anxious to meet any male bear. He could be especially hungry and might want her cubs for supper. Rather than try to defend them against the full-grown male ahead, she loped off in another direction. The cubs followed.

As they traveled along, a sudden spring storm filled the air with blowing snow. Forced to stop, the mother quickly dug a hole in a snowdrift, and the three bears huddled together in it until the blizzard ended.

When the family reached the sea ice, they were hungry. Finding seals would not be easy. Much walking and waiting would be necessary. They might wander hundreds of miles and spend most of their lifetime searching for seals.

This early in the spring most seals were swimming under the ice and surfacing only to breathe. To do this, the bullet-shaped seals had made holes in the ice by bashing their heads against it and gnawing it with their sharp teeth.

Chances were the mother bear wouldn't sight a seal the moment it surfaced. So before she could capture one, she had to locate its breathing hole which would still be covered with snow. But with her remarkable sense of smell the bear could scent a seal's exit hole with as much as four inches of snow piled upon it.

One day, as she hunted for seals, the mother bear climbed up a steep, icy ridge. Her huge paws, hairy soles, and sharp claws kept her from slipping on the ice. At the top she stood on her hind legs, craned her long neck, and looked about. As she sniffed the wind, she caught the scent of seal.

Quickly, she hid the cubs behind the ridge. Then she sneaked noiselessly across the ice below on her furred paws. Soon she spied a breathing hole. Carefully, she

moved against the wind so her own scent wouldn't blow toward the seal that might be surfacing any minute. Once at the seal's breathing hole, she tossed the top layers of the snow aside, and waited, lying flat on the nearby ice.

A seal below would have to come up to breathe in about seven minutes. Soon one popped up out of the hole. He sniffed the air and looked around. When he saw the bear's coal black nose, he dived down into the hole before she could pounce upon him.

Later that day, lying in wait at another breathing hole, the mother bear moved faster. As soon as she saw the ringed seal's dark shiny nose, she crushed his skull with one quick blow from her mighty paw.

Then she tore the seal apart and started to gorge herself on it. Every little while she left her feast and ambled to a nearby pool of water. There she washed her paws and face.

Midway through her meal, she tossed a few pieces of seal to her cubs. They licked the skin and sniffed at the blubber, but they still preferred their mother's milk.

Usually the blubber and a bit of the seal's skin satisfied the mother, but this time she also sampled some of the flesh. When she couldn't stuff any more into her stomach, shrunken from fasting, she and the cubs all took a nap together.

Ravens, circling in the sky all the while, swooped down and pecked at what remained of the seal.

Sometimes, as the mother bear hunted, the cubs played or strayed too close to a breathing hole and ruined her chance to grab a seal.

Meanwhile, with great grinding noises, fierce arctic winds and powerful currents began to break up the sea ice. Soon the sun began to melt the ice as well, opening up lanes of water.

One day the mother bear, traveling on an ice floe, let herself down backward into the icy water at the edge and coaxed her cubs to join her. They floated easily, aided by their dense fur and thick layer of fat.

To encourage them to swim, their mother ducked them a time or two. Then the cubs tried paddling with their forefeet and dragging their hindfeet. Their webbed toes helped them to swim.

When one cub tired, he grabbed his mother's tail and held on with his teeth, while she towed him through the water. Afterward, back on their ice floe, they all shook the water off their fur in doglike fashion.

Once accustomed to the water—so frigid that a man could live in it only a few minutes—the cubs swam more than their mother. On occasion they sprinted across the ice and dived into the water headfirst.

One afternoon the bears came to a channel. The mother leaped over it and waited for her cubs to swim across. Shortly after, they saw another bear family coming toward them. Silently, they ambled past each other on the ice. Afterward, the mother bear kept glancing back over her shoulder, anxiously watching the strangers until they disappeared from sight.

As seals began basking in the spring sun beside their breathing holes, now and then the mother bear caught one. But she wasn't capturing enough seals to satisfy her. So, one day as the cool, short arctic summer began, she jumped into the water and led her cubs toward another ice floe.

Suddenly, a churning of the water alarmed her. When she raised her head and looked around, she saw leaping black fins in the distance. A pack of killer whales was swimming in the open water ahead.

The mother bear knew that if a whale attacked her, she wouldn't have a chance. For a land animal she was a powerful swimmer, but in the water she was no match for the agile killer whale.

All she could do was rush back to the ice floe they had left. But what about her cubs? They couldn't keep up with her in the water.

Hurriedly, she urged them to climb upon her back. Then she swam as fast as she could until she reached their ice floe. Once there, she quickly shoved the cubs away from the edge of the ice.

They were still not entirely safe. If the whales had seen them and were extremely hungry, they might swim under the ice floe, break the ice by hitting it with their heads, and topple the bears into the water.

The bears were lucky this time. The whales turned toward a herd of swimming walrus and chased them instead.

As the bears hunted they rarely saw more than one seal basking near a breathing hole. But one day the mother saw three black blobs ahead. Every few seconds the sleepy seals tested the wind for bears and peered around for signs of danger.

Slowly and quietly the mother bear moved forward on her belly. Along the way she hid behind mounds of snow and when any of the seals stirred, she stopped.

When she was close enough, and the seals all seemed to be dozing, she sprang at them. Two seals quickly escaped down the breathing hole, but the mother bear grabbed the third, a hefty 200-pounder.

She and the cubs, now enjoying blubber as well as their mother's milk, ate well that day. As they expanded their diet, the cubs grew fast. Now about seven months old, they each weighed well over a hundred pounds.

One summer day a herd of walrus was swimming near the bears' ice floe. If the mother could catch one, they would have an enormous dinner.

She wouldn't dive into the water and attack a full-grown walrus. In the water the walrus was faster, and a well-aimed thrust of its long, powerful tusks could kill

the polar bear. Even if she attacked a calf she risked being gored, for the calf's mother and the rest of the herd would quickly come to its rescue.

Instead, the mother bear crouched on the edge of her ice floe and waited for a calf to come swimming along. When one did, she swatted at it with her immense paw. This time she missed, and the terrified calf raced back to its mother.

These days, as the sun melted more sea ice, it opened huge channels—sometimes more than a mile wide. Seals that now made their home in these channels had only to surface to breathe.

Seals swimming below the ice still needed to push themselves up through the ice to breathe. As the snow over their breathing holes melted, it was easier for the mother bear to find them. And her yellowish summer coat blended with the yellowish summer ice, making it harder for the seals to see her.

Many natural holes that a seal might use to breathe were also forming in the ice. Now and then the bear stretched

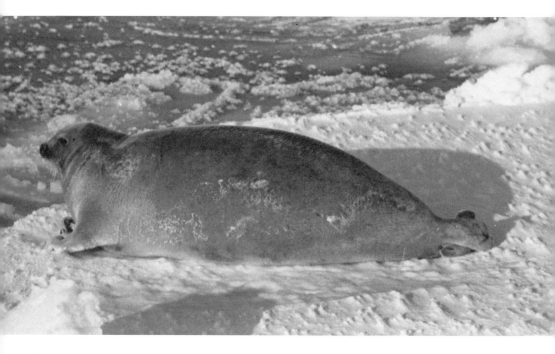

out near an unused hole and waited patiently for hours for a seal to appear.

Sometimes her cubs joined the hunt in their clumsy fashion. But they soon gave up and wandered away to play.

The mother bear kept trying new tricks to catch seals. Once, while the bears were swimming alongside an ice floe, the mother sighted a seal near the edge. Slowly the bear submerged, with only her black nose showing. She cruised along, hardly causing a ripple in the water. Once alongside the seal, she hurled herself out of the water and took a swift swipe at it. But the wary seal instantly dived into the water and escaped.

Another day, while on the ice, the mother bear saw a seal ahead napping beside its breathing hole. This time she swam underneath the hole and waited. When the seal dived into it, she grabbed him as he hit the water.

Some days the family roamed thirty miles over the ice without catching a seal. But when five days slipped by without their capturing a single seal, they swam ashore.

Then the three bears wandered along the coast. The top layer of this barren land, called tundra, had just thawed. The yellow arctic poppy was blooming, grass and moss carpeted much of the ground, and brightly colored lichens clung to the rocks. There were no trees; only dwarfed willows hugged the ground here and there.

On the land the hungry bears snacked on grasses, roots, and berries. The mother bear trapped lemmings beneath her paws and tossed them to her cubs. Along the seashore she dived for seaweed and gulped down parts of it.

At times the family lunched on eider duck. When the mother bear saw a flock swimming offshore she sank

gently below the waves. As she came up beneath one of the ducks, she snatched it.

The cubs tried to catch ducks, too, but they weren't skillful enough yet. Sometimes, however, they found nests of seabirds on the ground and gobbled up the eggs inside.

Meanwhile, their mother kept hunting for more filling meals. One day she saw a herd of musk ox on the tundra

grazing upon reindeer moss. She rarely stalked a full-grown ox, but after dining on tidbits, she was really hungry.

So she left the cubs waiting behind her and sneaked quietly toward a calf on the edge of the group. But the herd saw her approaching. Swiftly, to protect the calves, they formed a circle around them. The bear turned back rather than face all those menacing horns.

Soon the bear's scent led her to a free feast—a carcass of a white whale on the beach. When she reached it, more than thirty polar bears were already there. Some were ripping chunks of blubber from the whale. Some were entering it from a hole they had eaten in the belly and leaving by the mouth. Some were sleeping nearby after gobbling up as much as 150 pounds of blubber.

With plenty of food for all, none of the assembled bears showed any interest in the mother and her cubs as they joined the group and ate their fill.

As fall approached, the days grew colder. At night the northern lights flashed across the arctic sky in arcs of bright red, blue, and green.

Ice covered more of the sea, seals once again swam beneath the ice, and the bears returned to the sea ice.

As they hunted for seals, bushy-tailed arctic foxes followed them. Once the bears located a breathing hole, the foxes rested nearby. After the bears dined on seal, the foxes rushed over and gulped down the leavings.

This season the bears needed to eat heartily to build up reserves of fat for the harsh winter ahead. When they found the frozen carcass of a walrus, the bears ate until their bellies bulged. After they had feasted, gulls glided down and helped themselves.

Meanwhile as the bears hunted, the sun was setting earlier and earlier and rising later and later. The days were becoming very short. One night, about mid-November, the sun set for the last time. More than two months would pass before the bears would see the sun again.

It was seldom completely dark during this long polar night. The snow reflected light from the stars and the moon. And from below the horizon the sun's glow added a little light.

This winter the mother and her cubs remained on the sea ice. She slept in a den every third winter when she was expecting cubs. This year, like most bears except mothers-to-be, she sought only temporary shelter from the frigid winter.

At times heavy snow storms lashed the Arctic. While the blizzards raged, the mother and her cubs curled up together in a snowdrift.

This season the mother bear's coat changed to white, matching the white winter ice. Even so, she and her cubs found hunting seals harder than ever, as the seals' breathing holes were often buried under deep snow.

Life was harder for the foxes, too. More of them followed the polar bears, and the foxes were always close by, ready to devour what remained whenever the mother bear captured a meal.

In February the sun finally peeped above the horizon again. Before long seals would be plentiful, as seal pups joined the others. And as the snow gradually melted above their breathing holes they would be easier to find—if not to catch.

While seal-hunting one day the bears stopped to rest at the foot of an ice cliff. Soon the cubs began tumbling and somersaulting in the snow. They pretended to fight for awhile; then they grabbed and hugged each other.

As the family traveled again, the mother bear sniffed the wind. She caught the scent of huskies and dashed up the cliff, with the cubs following. From the top they could see dogs pulling Eskimo hunters on sleds. They were hunting seals, but a polar bear would be a real prize. The skin would bring them much money.

But neither the huskies nor the Eskimos could scale the steep, icy slope. And the white bear on the white ice wasn't an easy target. Still, one hunter fired a shot at the mother bear. It missed. Startled, the bears slid down the other side of the slope.

Another day the mother bear heard a droning sound in the distance. When she looked up, she saw a strange object in the sky. She was curious rather than afraid, so instead of galloping off with her cubs, she just stood and stared at the noisemaker as it came toward them.

As it flew directly above her, a man in the aircraft fired a dart containing drugs into the mother's rump. The frightened bear raced off in the rough ice and started up a ridge, before toppling over several minutes later.

The men in the helicopter were biologists tracking bears to learn more about them to help them survive.

After drugging the mother bear, they gave her a number. They tattooed this number inside her upper lip, added it to tags they fastened on her ears, and wrote it in purple

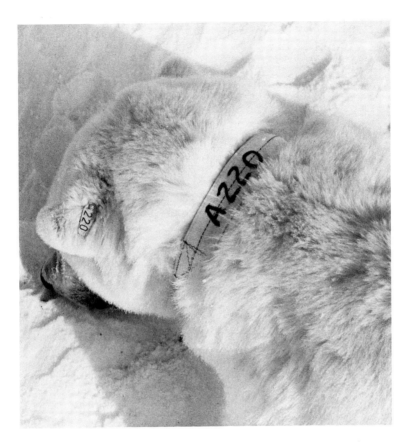

ink upon her back. A numbered collar, with a radio transmitter inside, was also fastened around her neck.

When she recovered, she stood on her hind legs and looked around anxiously for her cubs. When she saw them playing nearby, she hurried off to join them.

The cubs were now showing more interest than ever before in hunting. They dined mostly on seal, seldom drinking any of their mother's milk. By midsummer they weighed over two hundred pounds and were about five feet long.

Anytime that fall their mother might leave them. Instead, she kept caring for them and teaching them all she knew until they were about twenty-eight months old. Then one day the next spring, while the cubs were playing in the snow, she just loped off, never even glancing back over her shoulder.

She met an adult male bear on the sea ice that spring, mated again, and gave birth to cubs in her winter den—twins once more. She would live another twenty years at the top of the world.

The cubs she abandoned stayed together for awhile. Together or apart, they faced severe hazards, which only experience and growth would help them conquer.

In time they mastered many ways to hunt seals. They gained the strength needed to defend themselves against

adult bears. They learned to detect the scent of hunters and to hide from them. And finally, like all other polar bears, they became the undisputed animal rulers of the arctic ice.

# ABOUT THE AUTHOR

Kay McDearmon was born in San Francisco and received her B.A. degree from the University of California at Berkeley. Before devoting her time to writing, she was a high school teacher and social service worker.

In addition to her present book on the polar bear, she is the author of A DAY IN THE LIFE OF A SEA OTTER, THE WALRUS: GIANT OF THE ARCTIC ICE, and MAHALIA, GOSPEL SINGER.

Kay McDearmon lives with her husband, a professor of Speech Pathology, in Turlock, California, where leisure time activities include bicycling, swimming, reading, and music.

c.1